THE SITUATION

Also by John Skoyles

Poetry:
A Little Faith
Permanent Change
Definition of the Soul

Prose:
Generous Strangers
Secret Frequencies: A New York Education

THE SITUATION

poems by
JOHN SKOYLES

Carnegie Mellon University Press
Pittsburgh 2007

Acknowledgments

Grateful acknowledgment is made to editors of the following
magazines in which these poems first appeared:

The Antioch Review: "Aisle 8"

The Atlantic Monthly: "Uncle Grossman," "The Situation,"
    and "Lottery"

Italian Americana: "The Boy Whose Parents Drink" and "Giovanni
    Bertolotti"

Orion: "Lilacs"

Poetry: "Academic," "I Dreamt I Went to Hell Charles Schwab,"
    and "Uncle Dugan"

River City: "The Daughters of the Ticket Taker"

Slate: "Three Shards"

TriQuarterly: "Fishing," "In the Radiation Oncology Waiting
    Room," "No Name for It," and "The Wish Mind"

Washington Square: "After Petrarch"

"Academic" also appeared in *The Poetry Anthology: Ninety Years of
America's Most Distinguished Verse Magazine.*

The publication of this book is supported by a
grant from the Pennsylvania Council on the Arts.

Library of Congress Control Number: 2006924989
ISBN-13: 978-0-88748-472-8
ISBN-10: 0-88748-472-7

10   9   8   7   6   5   4   3   2   1

Contents

for Emilia

I

Lottery

Pick a number,
any number,
and it will bear
the teeth marks of time.
The day confetti
stippled your shoulders
to keep love
bright and alive;
the year your newborn
son survived.
The two of us riding
the 33 bus
to the birthday bash
where a prophetic
blues band played
"You've Changed."
The magnificent sum
of always, now and still
dealt by the god
who pinched fate
into every living vein.

The Wish Mind

Eternity might very well
be the longed for kiss
you wish would stop,
or the brazen ambition
to live with god,
now folded in the churchyard
with the horse chestnuts.

Eternity could simply
be the thirty shots of radiation
that took you thirty times
until the ending didn't finish,
nor the beginning start.

A girl pats her forehead
with a powder puff,
as if dotting the letter i.
She becomes an x, you change
to o, and the infinite game
ends always in a tie.

Eternity might take the shape
of a werewolf in the wish mind.
The librarian bends over
to look up a skirt.
The howl is strong
and we hear it forever.

Or maybe it's the dominating
see-saw in the center
of the playground,
whose rusty fulcrum squeals
to the children:
Life is long, William.
Life is short, Kate.

No Name for It

A full shot glass in the desert,
shimmering on the bar of the Mirage.

An aged singer back on her feet,
dressed in gold like an autumn leaf.

Someone covers your eyes from behind,
a kindred sport waiting for his change.

It's before soon and after late,
John Gerard,

when you spurn the stiff lie
of sobriety, and your soul lifts

from its trustworthy script.
The blind greeting, jocular and kind,

asks a question you can't answer
Mr. S.,

and because you cannot guess
who's there,

you do not guess.

Whisper

A steady whisper asks
"What's wrong with Paul?"
while we shuffle the deck
that deals one hand the queen
and jack, ten, nine, eight.
There's laughter at the lucky
straight, and elbows bend
until it's time to leave
our friend with the phrase
he learned today, medical for fate.
He touches us as we've
been touched by the blade
of moon hanging overhead.
What's wrong with Paul?
What's wrong? Those words
call like the song of quail,
cathedral bells, two taps
of a fist against a closed door.

Elegy

It wasn't from age
because he rose to greet it.
We ruled out love
since he was known to fear it.
It wasn't the tumor
because he beat it.
And yet the years
of strain and flail
leaned together
and took the blame
for easing his face
from the mirror,
his weight off the scale.
He chose to be found
on the pine needle floor
where he cut cords
and heard the hermit thrush
sing like broken glass
falling to the street,
like the churning sting
of the sweet pink drink
his mother stirred
in a childhood swirl.
The cascading drawl
of the hidden bird
followed the cursive
of his name on the note
he left behind
to his place in the row
engraved in stone.

After a Death

The merciful cushion
of early dark,
the banshee dusk
and waterfall roar
of a steel shaker
draining ice,
the night, the gin,
the FM station's
sanctimonious violin
call to life
the one who died.
His mourners share
a pain so great
they speak the same
and sit together
knee to knee,
the hand of hurt youth
on the arm of the old country.
We walk his wife
across the lawn
where an orange moth,
a sister underwing,
shifts in the black-gowned breeze
as it curtsies to each soul
on the top rung of grief.

In the Hospital

The bleating petals of the lily,
the inchworm on a stamen
drifting by a thread,
the near symmetry
of a rolled-up paper ball,
the visitor's three-dimensional
vertical life,
all seem impossible
to one who lies on his side.
Every story ends
the same —
and then he died —
though prayers beg
the tale to go
beyond the grave
where putrefaction
and decay
might very well
pray themselves,
but are most surely
twirling through remains
regardless of the lily's call,
the inchworm's instinct
to sit up and flail,
and the ingenious paper ball's
declaration of love
thought better of.

Apostrophe S

Fragrance does not wear fragrance,
it owes its breath

to the thin sheen
perfume brings to the neck

where possession
is more than nine-tenths

of the law.
Or it binges alone

on a mirrored tray
arranged by size and shape,

waiting for its chance
to charge the brain

with the kind
of change

a bevy of handkerchiefs
can't wave clean.

Violets, lilacs,
lilies of the valley,

which do you call yours?
Drivers and pedestrians

pass the same stuttering
shops, the lunch place,

a butterfly bush
adorned by wings,

and the dog sleeping
on the oak's curled roots

who doesn't doubt
he'll always rise

at the sound of his name.

Ash

It could have been you,
father of two, who choked
in Truro in an alcoholic hollow.
A finger writes his name in dust
and when those syllables sound,
the consonants and vowels
clown around in stories
of his special way
of never saying no
to his lazy basset hound
or to the boys
now shot with pain
from the prism that pins
all those who lose
their fathers young.
In some part of their hearts
they continue to believe
in the immortality
of pets and ghosts and god,
and that the stray cylinder
of ash rolling on the floor
from their father's
four-pack-a-day life
has a word for them,
a word still left to say.

Ledger

Rolling Dice, Higher Power,
Unmoved Mover,
one of them

dropped this ice
down our backs,
dusted the dates

on gravestones,
the parenthesis
trailing us home

from work
to the window
where we stare at the storm

that arrived like a tap
on the shoulder
from a disappearing stranger.

No one's there
except a solitary
stitched to a tall drift.

Inside, the armchairs
fill with household goblins
drawing up a will.

To this one, that.
To that one, this.
To him who lost

two wives,
the arias and soundtracks.
To her, the dog

and his snarling view
of the bone.
And the forbidden couch

to our crying Siamese
so he can share
with the moth

the velvet cushions
pressed into dust
by the guests

who have left.

Academic

I see straight through myself
and into the no mirror.

A frame stares back,
announcing the time: late.
And the temperature:
still warm.

I recognize the calm
bystander's snowy face,
the handwriting on the blackboard

where chalk dust
from the names of the present
falls to the ledge
toward those who have disappeared.

Song of the Lost and Found

Where does the weight
of the cut branch go
when it returns as driftwood
to the squalling beach?

Do lilies know they last
just a day?

Is the mockingbird praying
for a voice of his own,
or does he rejoice
that worms are blind?

If you find your pen
in the lost and found,
your dog in the pound,
a strong friend
under a mound of clay
too soon,
what do you say?

Time's a wick, a fuse,
a trick to see
if you can shake off
loss and claim,
and dance in pain?

Fishing

I put down the phone and decide
to go fishing,
tired of the noise in my hand.

The rod is ready. Line spins
toward the charging sky
and into the pockmarked sea.

The silver lure thinks everyone has a price.

The fish say the price today is too high.

The sun remains neutral.
Its fight is with the earth
over who will last longer.

I cast and cast into the celestial drink
while the voice of the beyond
speaks through the tide.

I remain on shore
but divide from the man
wiping the sun from his skin
with a heartsick flag.

One side of the brain
hears sadness
in the tingling buoys.
The other says: don't project.

I stand back
and perform that cruel gymnastic
for the soul:
I take a good look at myself.

And I begin to laugh
until I am whole again,
until I know it's not funny.

Great Hollow Beach

We walk the beach
at dead low,
when the climbing sea
is flattened to a breeze

and we are free
to approach the horizon,
the edge we bought
to feel the flick

of its blade
at our leisurely throats.
Along the cliff,
live sand

swallows the unwary,
unlike the corners
and cross streets
that eat life in inches.

The spiritual world
is invisible tonight
unless you believe
god draws

in big garish swipes
that leave us staring
at the sky,
the blond figure

down the beach,
and a corvette
from New Jersey
the color of a dragonfly.

Three Shards

At certain times of day
the lure displays itself
too loudly. Too proud
the triple treble hooks,
too bright the lacquered
shank of snare
flashing through a school
of bass, an invitation
pressed and passed.
At times like this,
it's best to join those
collecting stones
and shells and sticks,
reminders that
we won't survive
even as we resist
the pull to go beyond
where we belong,
like fish.
Flat stones taken home,
no voice or song,
but strong, heavy playing cards
facedown on a shelf
for us to touch in comfort,
not alarm — for that,
we have the phone
whose ring at certain times
means just one thing.

II

Thou Sayest

With winter came surprising deaths
and the predictable obituaries
of those closer to stone
than to breath.

The deepest snow does not ask the plow,
thou sayest.

Rope saved to hang himself,
a pack of leggy cards —
these secrets broke
from my neighbor's chest of drawers
when he dropped
between a shovel and a pail of salt.

We watch them die until we die, thou sayest.

Parallel rows in the snow
from the unlifted feet of the old,
craters in the script of their signatures . . .

We only live so long with those we love,
thou sayest.

I've got a lovely bunch of coconuts,
my mother chirps at the bars of a keet cage,
Roll-a, bowl-a, ball-a-penny-a-pitch,
my father replies from his spot in the shade.

A bleached nurse praises
their joyful way
of counting back from a hundred.

They're yours until you think they're mine,
thou sayest.

The Garden

She's been dead nine days
and tonight a phantom
bends its shade
across her jewelry box
with the same
concentrated stare
as when she sorted through
the spare parts of luxury,
but the shadow chooses
costume rings she'd never wear.
Will he embrace this wraith
festooned with her bracelets
and perfume?
He will, as he welcomes
the weight of a single
long blond hair
on the shoulder of his shirt.
A summer fog slides through
the garden, the right
atmosphere for spirits
to lead an ectoplasmic trek
across the fireworks
of evening primrose
and honeysuckle.
Children on the street sing
a lilting dirge involving worms
and a mahogany box,
the same grain as the bed
where they exchanged
both soft and burly breaths.
From the bedroom
he can see the compost hill
that feeds the lilies
with its breathing hump

that almost sniffles in the heat,
a distraction until she appears
again. Brown in summer.
In winter, white.

Lilacs

We call their scent unworldly
though all scent is earth-bred:

the perfumed parade down Fifth,
the dog's shoulder

flounced against the carcass
of a fox.

Fuming branches
near the flagstones

transform the wind
the way a shy mouth

puckers in the snap
of pleasure.

Lilacs owe their lives
to the rain and sun,

and when there's thunder
at the door,

they enter
without knocking.

The Boy Whose Parents Drink

The boy whose parents drink
brings a favorite toy
to the lull
between the aimed cup
and the tea-stained wall.
He stands on the carpet
holding a ball that blinks,
a light he thinks will calm the room.

The boy whose parents drink
leaves broken glass
in the school mail slot
then bangs his forehead
on the floor,
hard and harder
for bigger laughs.

The boy whose parents drink
is called to pick the one
he'll live with:
the father who pounds out
light bulbs with his fist,
or the mother whose shelf
of knick-knacks tumbles
when she clips her crystal
with a countering swipe.

The boy whose parents drink
misses drinking
with his drinking father,
just a sip.
As his father opens the car door,
the boy whose parents drink
says, *Bye, Dad* over and over

until nightfall,
when he lies in bed
and makes deals
with the ceiling.

The boy whose parents drink
gets his wish
and does so well in math
a leaning teacher
beams over him
while the class lines up.
Pointing to the zero,
the boy whose parents drink
climbs through it and disappears.

Mrs. Bristol and the Sailor

What loosened the dusk
like a prying light?
The bright curve
of a clamshell drive
biting the land
over my shoulder.
And that fire
across the harbor
by the tall stone tower,
is it the purifying blaze
of a leaf-piled lawn,
or something smaller?
Perhaps a sailor
cupping a match
in his fist,
igniting a cigarette
for Mrs. Bristol . . .
Does she lean on his knee?
Is she the same Mrs. Bristol
of the famed Bristol-Myers,
and is my father the sailor?
Yes. Because this is not distance
but the distant past,
where I see through
the eyes of a man
turned shutterbug of memory.
Mrs. Bristol is nothing to look at,
but hops atop his lap
and says, *I like Navy men.*
My father's flame
nudges the taut fog
like the sharp elbow
of the driveway's chipped bone,
and there's a kind of kiss
I still hear in a strong wind.

Speak

Speak, but not like the dog
who gives a paw,
the mongrel with the megaphone
circling his neck to keep him
from his hip's stitched wound.
Don't speak like perfume,
that oxymoronic chloroform
of drizzle and downpour.
Speak like a fireman speaks
with his axe, like Lazy Mary
when asked to wash up.
Speak from deep
in your sloping throat,
whose curve evokes both love and war.
Speak like a tomahawk
and crossbow,
stun gun and Remington.
Speak like the founder
of a new religion,
its bishop and its sexton.
Mop the chapel's aisles
and slap the soldiers in Christ's army
with the chrism of salvation.
Summon the stamina to speak
for the children who stood
by chalkboards for spelling bees,
and the two times two
catastrophes that always sent
someone screaming from the room.
Let's follow him, the one who fled
but wailed out loud against
the ancient battle-axe and prim cuckoo.

St. Bartholomew's Church

Our lips in the waxy chapel air
address stained-glass angels
in the apse and a saint
displaying knives that flayed

him alive. A woman
set for the beach has already
applied oil mixed with iodine.
And my grandmother entering

the church brings the scent
of ancient parmesan,
transferred from her palm
to her black dress and purse.

We stand and kneel and sing
under the steeple where god
is nothing more than god,
but man is more than man

because he talks to those not there.
Or is god rousing our mouths
in a creed from the hymnal
through his ventriloquist's sleeve?

Giovanni Bertolotti

1876–1928

My mother's hand, a cursive trained by nuns,
wrote, "Found downstairs — you can discard"
across the packet of her father's death:

obit, vital certificate, little filler
from the *Mirror's* back pages —
flint phrases yanked from a trough

of stiff-brimmed prose and the doleful tones
of a medical examiner. No word of wife
or child, just that he fell six flights

from his perch on a scaffold.
Rain brings out a roofer's best and worst
and my mother once drew for us the pitch

of the sugar refinery's tall boiler house,
where a shining statue of Jack Frost
pranced the sky in a pointy hat,

tossing handfuls of pure granules
from a pouch. Should I describe
my grandmother's life, left with eight kids?

Instead I'll end with the snow-white sprite
who did not become "a victim of the weather,"
as the tabloid's squib portrayed

this immigrant leaving his beginnings
near Rome only to land in a railroad car
of pig iron in Edgewater, N. J.,

a town consigned to have its losses
sweetened by an elf, from bay
to bridge, from street to sister street.

The Ghost of Emma Lazarus

As you know, ghosts float and blow
with the wind, so when she died,
her soul looked down on the city
and cried the cry of a single thread
that longed to be used by a bird
for its nest, but instead found itself
sewn to the vest of a three-piece suit.
She passed cafes where fragrance
met arrogance, eyebrows tweezed
into the high feigned surprise
of those who leave their lives in mirrors.
Emma traveled near and far
but it took a ghost to show her
that her pen welcoming the poor
would begin the same story
again and again against the backdrop
of asphalt, steel and brick,
relieved now and then
by a phosphorescent gleam
that made breathing a sky
of ash just fine, that made rising
every day from the subway
like creatures from a lake
an okay way to make a living.
On the corner of MacDougal
near the park, she overheard
children at games invented
for their lack of gear.
A girl leans her forehead
to a fence and counts by fives
then looks for those with no place to hide.

Symptomatic

Pleased simply to recall
the chestnuts
gathered in a pall of rain.

Happy just to breathe a bit
the fragrance
that we once consumed.

Can you live with this,
the voices running toward you
from a glass of wine,
the rinsings of the past?

Do you secretly envy
the rush of fisticuffs
near the bar door,
the world of flying forearms,

the men and women
who thunder their way,
while the rest mull the paths
their lives became?

Wouldn't you want to see once more
the rows of corn on Wunderstrand Farm,
the clouds above a boxcar
that jumped the track?

Ladies and gentlemen of the jury,
what is the word for regret?

The Daughters of the Ticket Taker

Snowflakes ambushed the mourners,
the daughters of the ticket taker,
while a family of crows
drowned out their chattering hurt.
The youngest, in a tender dress,
closed her eyes
against the sharp-shooting dazzle.
Her name was Autumn,
we used to say hello,
but I never dreamt
that when they buried her father,
the bent man who tore
tickets at the Jackson,
I'd be taking a walk
through the ample parenthesis
of St. Samuel's cemetery,
toward that smaller pause
between Autumn's cupped hands.

Loves Me Not

It's raining on the brain turmoil
where sick cells ring
with the sound of a matchstick
stuck in a doorbell.

It rains on the hospital roof,
along headlines
in the waiting room
where the boiling aquarium

flips silver hatchet fish
under the wheels of the gurney.
And it rains on the alibi
of the boy on the front page,

a trickling path mixed with pain.
Water glass, bedpan,
raindrops on a window
never troubled by a brain,

cord with a squeeze bulb
that sucks the universe
toward life's she-loves-me,
loves-me-not.

In the Radiation Oncology Waiting Room
Massachusetts General Hospital

With my small problem, I'm like the vandal
jailed for carving nicknames on a bench
while the rest are facing heavier time.
We stare at the aquarium's
cruel centerpiece of brain coral,
and the brass plaque memorializing,
of all names, Tom Dooley.
Why is the girl in the red sweatshirt crying?
Her mother's hand softly touches her hood,
and softly her small brother scans the room,
unmoved, until the explanations come.
Volunteers offer juice or music,
and the man beside me wears a shirt
that would go unnoticed anywhere but here,
So many books, so little time . . .
A patient grabs a rushing doctor by the wrist,
forcing his pain into phrases
honed to snare the man of science.
My neighbor taps his book
and says, "I can't put it down,"
because he needs to know the ending,
unlike the other endings here,
still mysterious, still unsolved.
For the very ill, there's hope
in simple words that signify
the simplest future,
so when the man in a gown
extends directions to his seaside home,
we picture it before us,
the highway and the bridge,
the exit curving to land's end,
the turn at the overflowing forsythia
that no one's missed yet.

Prayer Without a God

I'm not your sparrow,
Father X,
though I've been scuffing
patio dust
while you majestically
direct the bees
through swollen lilac sprigs.
Bad god, jaunty god
all-knowing but forgetful god
of the fractious millimeters
that grow on the brain
without purpose
but change everything,
this is to remind you
I'm still here,
drinking gin in a lawn chair
at gorgeous dusk,
just a twitch of sorrow
because you promised
to notice every sparrow,
and then ignored
the accelerating tumor
and the glass sky
that blinds
the ounce of feathers
to its own reflection.

Something

In every thought there's spring and fall,
and between each heartbeat,
a stopped watch
nudged along.
In every face, a rising sun
and coming dark,
and in every soul,
a thing that outsmarts
off and on.
Tattoos say you were born
to lose, the thing says
you'll just fade away.
There's a tap on your shoulder,
a ship in your heart,
and something taking you
the way of everyone
who ever rented room
in dreams come true.
Torn from childhood,
born again mid-life,
and toward the end
you learned to live
with the old man
who follows every
wedding on the street,
and can't take his eyes
off the satin bride
stained white.

The Healer

The healer said look inward
at the pain, and see
how firm or bright or loud.
I found a garden in full term,
a path of fronds and flowers
leading to the tumor chewed
by rays but still unfazed
and changed into a lily
fanged with petals
so grotesquely whorled
it's called the Scatterbrain.
Is this what the healer
had in mind,
to find a vaudevillian
in a killer's trance?
I kept up the drill,
my fate fused with this face
that breathed a scent
so strong from summer warmth
I heard bees humming
"The Night They Invented Champagne,"
and watched a jacket
flying on a nearby line,
one sleeve blown
across the collar
as if shielding its sight
from danger above or below.
In tumor town, you never
know what's next.

The Situation

It's tough, isn't it, star,
to be harangued
by every strain
of brimming heart?

It's hard, isn't it, moon,
when crowds fidget
with their swizzle sticks
as you brighten the bay?

And head, doesn't it hurt
when love ignites
its pesky orbit
and all logic strays?

Hot, isn't it, sun?

Admit it's a relief, shade,
to wear camouflage
while the flamboyant
fade away.

Go ahead, god,
and blame this mess
of blood
and flesh on free will.

That's life, isn't it, death,
when guardrails
along the steep drive home
bristle with wreaths and bouquets?

III

I Dreamt I Went to Hell
With Charles Schwab

He promised me a sail on his Swan
but off the bay
he steered wrong
and soon we faced a fork
swung by the Dark One.
Charles had the tender jowls
of a new senator,
no rent worries ever pitched
their tents there,
packed up, pitched again.
The greasy, dented cheeks of Satan
mirrored my own lumped
and pointy features, no symmetry.
He asked us to explain who had touched
our lives, moved us most, fathered
our fates, the friends who failed us.
Charles confessed first: he never
had a second thought, just pounced.
As for me, I had only second thoughts,
and therefore never . . .
For these crimes
we were condemned
to fathom each other through a kiss.
Charles understood me right away:
burnt coffee, aspirin, envy.
The rich man tasted familiar, like sucking
a penny, a miniature copper mine,
blood from a fishhook wound,
and the fish, and the hook, and the wound.

Uncle Dugan

A van knocked down the kid playing tag.
The rest of us stood on a manhole cover
above Brooklyn's slurring waste
and beneath the elevated train

that sawed the sun and moon in two.
The driver waved a fifth
of Four Roses like a bad wand
and we disappeared

while tenements emptied to the curb
where Alice Gallon sang "Chantilly Lace"
until her mother slapped
her face with a sauce spoon

with some tomato sauce still on it.
I went home to parts of a steer
bobbing in broth, and Uncle Dugan
exhaling Pall Malls toward

the teardrop chandelier and drinking
Heaven Hill from the bottle.
He said one law demands we eat well
but another keeps food from the poor,

that I was lucky I stayed put
on the iron disk
above Smith Street's suds and shit,
but should know

that even though I'm safe
before a placemat and a spoon,
no drink or art is strong enough
to undermine the fact

that every victim
once inhabited the crowd
of witnesses like you
and you and you.

Uncle Grossman

Uncle Grossman quotes the Greeks and the gods
and says the Great One knows when a feather
falls to a field, then he clears his throat
with the sound of a brake yanked into place.
Grossman, our childless nuncle, bumps
his avuncular head hard against the bird feeder.
As seed fills his fedora's rim, he says,
*Pain makes a world that would not exist
except for pain.* On the way to dinner,
Uncle Grossman describes his current loves,
a woman with five bulldogs, and the nurse
who sneaks him endless Xanax.
Life is comic, he says, *and life is tragic.*
Uncle G. orders his favorite dish, Veal P.,
but does not recommend it.
Although our uncle has not been born again,
he booms with the strength of the just born
against white chocolate, the rosary,
and Galileo's fate. When a small nephew
asks us to drive faster, his uncle states,
*No matter how many cars you pass,
you cannot pass the car ahead of you.*
It's a rainy evening when we see him to the bus.
The long aisle of windows steams,
and we wave goodbye to Uncle Grossman
through the little circle of clarity
he keeps rubbing clean with the heel of his fist.

I Think Continually of Those
Not Asked to Dance

I think continually
of those not asked to dance:
the blossoms yearning
in magnolia trees,
the sleek stockings
of the waitress
standing on a stool
to change a dying bulb,
the pink-white petal in her hair
eloped from the row
on Commonwealth
to the parade
of flesh and blood below.
The daring flower dares
all hands to tilt
toward her pulled-back part,
but as she stretches higher
I board a train
that climbs straight up
her nylon seam.
No conductor takes tickets
or calls out the stop
for the Tea for Two Cafe,
so I am far away
when she steps down
and the wayward petal
see-saws to the floor.
We watch it fall,
those who found life
in that silken wing,
while she looks at us
with the same grave face
she gave the flickering light
before it died.

Ghazal: My Way

An empty dinghy called *The Crouton* drifts our way.
The boy swimming after it hears us pointing out its way.

I stagger from the blanket we set neatly in the sand
and wade into the ocean that takes our breath away.

I rethink my marriage, the time of day, our children
clawing at the blisters on their legs, the jam we put away

in early morning which now gushes from the bread,
and for a second I feel an ache for shore, but I'm carried away

by a crazy wanderlust for the tides of yesterday, when a sleek girl
poured tequila, scattered salt around our wrists and said *let's get away*

from here, but I didn't go, I stayed as if an anchor or a pier
held me in place, unlike finding myself out deep, going every which way

after the dinghy, when I used to have big dreams: ocean liners,
ports of call, an at-your-service captain in the gangway.

Then I'm distracted by a glamorous kite that seems to enjoy
being shaken through the sky, going the wind's way

with abandon, fighting the pull that binds it to the hand.
And I feel rivaled by the lost boat, the feisty kite, and regret my way

has always been to stay on shore, until now when I jumped
to help track down the dinghy that drifted away,

leaving me in freezing water, holding a rope, saying, *John,*
John, you're talking to yourself again, the coward's way.

Aisle 8

I lift a banged can
in the aisle of banged cans,

and a shape stares back,
a face I recognize,

someone I've seen
maneuvering

crumpled aluminum
tons at the dump,

a punch-drunk
heavyweight

led by his father
who escorts the ruined giant

everywhere,
to get the paper,

a bag of grass,
his son still trying to duck

a hemorrhaging past
as he suddenly drops low

at the newsstand.
His head wanders

above his body
like the splayed skull

of a dinner plate dahlia
in the fall wind.

And though it may be ugly,
a fumbled label

in a label-proud world,
it holds a torn corner

of truth, and begins to sing:
If you love me, say so.

If you don't love me, say so.
If you love me and are afraid

to say so, squeeze out my story,
but don't keep me waiting

in this cold convulsive light too long,
because here comes the night-man.

After Petrarch

Some animals
face the sun all day.

Light hurts the rest
who only come out at evening.

Then there's the strange throng
that loves fire

because it has the inexplicable allure
of being fickle.

Sorry to say,
I'm with them,

a shadow's slave
not strong enough

to see beyond the glamour
of danger.

And I can't seem to hide
my fugitive

in late hours,
and I can't tell

whose beautiful legs
those are

behind Chris.

Warmest Personal Regards

Above her name
on the note,
she wrote
Warmest Personal Regards.
Seven syllables,
ignoring my want
of her,
and my will.
Warm, Warmer,
Warmest —
no matter how I stretch it,
it turns out
like the white walls
of my bedroom
where vitreous floaters
go insane,
and her perfume
makes a museum
of the pillowcase.
All this
come about
from her name
on the note.

Tinnitus

Not the ocean's stutter in a storm,
but the tunneling
of sullen low-tide crabs
lisping Velásquez, Vichyssoise,
Chardonnay and Charlemagne —
a chorus kept in time
by the metronomic ping
of a pong ball
against plate glass
about to loosen
in its frame.
And when you think
it can't get worse,
there's the thip and click
of TV trays unfolding
onto the dewy
wall-to-wall in 1958
as Perry Como sings
his theme designed to lift
each soul from its swamp,
"Dream Along with Me
I'm on my Way to a Star."

Gardenia

When the girl with the combs
lets her hair
flank the shoulder of the one
who holds her hand;
when flat clouds pass
wand-like, yet nothing
changes the expression
on your heart-shaped face;
before I read too much
into beach fronds
flapping like semaphores
and find the bottom
of the glass looking up;
when I ask my collection
of keepsakes to shake off
their graves and dance:
pinecone, split stone,
ashtray saying
Dubo Dubon Dubonnet,
and from a dead aunt,
the tarot deck
I cut right now,
a gardenia appears
behind the ear of a woman
who holds a finger to her lips.
Don't let her stop you.
Tell me.

Initials Written on a Screen Door in Dew

Ask me whose name it is,
and why I remember
her little wave, a kind of smile,
and then the pert turned up
pleat of her skirt
flicking the rest of the street away.
Engines and motors were speaking
in tongues, and litter scribbled
leaves along the curb.
Minutes before, she savored
the sheen of a fancy shop,
the only time she glanced
expensive air.
Smooth hairbrush, boar bristles,
what every woman wants —
Freudians, now you know!
In her absence,
everything seemed something else,
and a jet crossed the absolute
like a tiny crucifix
leaving behind
a stark pew of believers.

In the Air

I turned pages on the plane
until I became a book

where your name and mine
crowned a fictional family tree,

a list of invisible progeny
we hatched in the happy hour

of a downtown bar,
the great blotto machine

that led us to children
we said we would love,

but did not love enough
to escort from the dark.

I picture them beside me,
initialing the cold pane

with fingerprints,
their faces mottled

with the tints and shades
of lost hope.

From the window along the wing,
a torn cloud dampens

the steel sheen.
I might have nodded off,

but I was pulsing havoc
from where I hung in the air,

watching the parade below
march so musically

across our teeming ball of clay,
my eyes wide

with the stare of a child
lifted above

the rosy, fecund, decked-out couples,
while a voice asked,

See? See? Can you see?

Nothing More

In the back of the cab
I found a badge,
a fake star
to scare the pants off
people already scared.
And flashing that spark
in the woolen dusk,
I said what I could
never say by day,
that I miss your spry
untimely touch,
the way our breathing
tangled and unfurled.
I said, *I would* . . .
but you kissed me with a kiss
even a heartsick
lack love would ignore,
a consolation kiss, the kiss you whisk
your sister on Christmas,
a kiss that promised nothing,
approached on a small drift
and sailed through the uprights,
tying the score.
Then the avenue seemed darkest,
the stoplights scarlet,
and our driver,
neither priest nor witness,
as you opened the door.

Fate

In the fortune-telling cards
spinning toward annihilation,
there lives a ghost
of a chance.

Sometimes we call it optimism.
Sometimes fate.

Either way, we say
Everything happens for the best.

The field goes to seed
and blows across time.
A farmer bends toward his son
under friendly, puffy gods in gauze.

Soon it will rain and, for a moment,
you feel rage is reversible,
that you can suddenly
convince A
to escape with you to Z.

So this is your legacy,
these are the cards you drew:

A love that wooed you to the brink.
There will be talk.
Time cures all,
except for what it doesn't cure.

Two Weeks in August

Don't say the waves
keep bullying the shore,
waves are afraid of themselves,

as you have been afraid
in those days
when love and hate

were the rage,
you heard sharp talking
at your back,

and a smile twisted its curve
as you walked past the dunes,
the steep climb, the low pools

with their surprises,
the little girl leaning over
a shallow rink of slime

who twirls a parasol
and names the creatures
seeking new shells.

The tide retreats,
the land ricochets
from day to day.

The shore is signed
with names of all kinds,
and years go by.

Here Comes One Now

The harbor exults in its glamour
on those evenings
when a dragger's leaky crankcase

varnishes the bay,
but at clarifying dawn
a parade of pasty faces unrolls

in a slow incontrovertible sheen.
Here comes one now,
the girl with hair

the color of copper wire
who practices pouting her coffee mouth.
And there goes that pall of a man

whose happiest years have passed,
and once in a while
a phantom arrives,

the suicide who falls victim
to a sea that throws itself
in front of him.

And here comes the shipped-out
sailor's wife, shopping for a chain,
and there's the spot on the dock

where a kid cut his head
and the whole pier
called for a cop.

Here comes one now,
followed by another,
tromping down the boardwalk
toward our blood-wet boy.

Addendum

I don't have any secrets
unless she was my secret
that summer of rain
the hydrangeas gained weight,
and tourists walked the shore

in shorts eaten by moths,
the shaggy pets of summer's hearth.
To her, summer was a simple
addendum to the overworked year.
A porch. A reaching out,

an act of pity granted
by the god of summer.
But pity, like a summer kiss,
like a kiss on the porch
in summer,

and the porch itself,
extends just so far.
Twin insomniacs hijacked
my sleep that summer:
one who snapped

at the purring brain;
the other who planned
a change at summer's end
and blinked like phosphor
through the clenching dark.

I don't have any secrets
unless she was my secret
that month I rode a drop of rain

down her freckled back
as it fled the summer.

Standing under an awning,
why did everyone running by
seem lost,
and summer so long?
And summer so very long?

Previous Titles in the
Carnegie Mellon Poetry Series:
2000–2007

2000
Small Boat with Oars of Different Size, Thom Ward
Post Meridian, Mary Ruefle
Hierarchies of Rue, Roger Sauls
Constant Longing, Dennis Sampson
Mortal Education, Joyce Peseroff
How Things Are, James Richardson
Years Later, Gregory Djanikian
On the Waterbed They Sank to Their Own Levels, Sarah Rosenblatt
Blue Jesus, Jim Daniels
Winter Morning Walks: 100 Postcards to Jim Harrison, Ted Kooser

2001
The Deepest Part of the River, Mekeel McBride
The Origin of Green, T. Alan Broughton
Day Moon, Jon Anderson
Glacier Wine, Maura Stanton
Earthly, Michael McFee
Lovers in the Used World, Gillian Conoley
Sex Lives of the Poor and Obscure, David Schloss
Voyages in English, Dara Wier
Quarters, James Harms
Mastodon, 80% Complete, Jonathan Johnson
Ten Thousand Good Mornings, James Reiss
The World's Last Night, Margot Schilpp

2005

Laws of My Nature, Margot Schilpp
Things I Can't Tell You, Michael Dennis Browne
Renovation, Jeffrey Thomson
Sleeping Woman, Herbert Scott
Blindsight, Carol Hamilton
Fallen from a Chariot, Kevin Prufer
Needlegrass, Dennis Sampson
Bent to the Earth, Blas Manuel De Luna

2006

Burn the Field, Amy Beeder
Dog Star Delicatessen: New and Selected Poems 1979–2006,
    Mekeel McBride
The Sadness of Others, Hayan Charara
A Grammar to Waking, Nancy Eimers
Shinemaster, Michael McFee
Eastern Mountain Time, Joyce Peseroff
Dragging the Lake, Robert Thomas

2007

So I Will Till the Ground, Gregory Djanikian
Trick Pear, Suzanne Cleary
Indeed I Was Pleased With the World, Mary Ruefle
The Situation, John Skoyles
One Season Behind, Sarah Rosenblatt
The Playhouse Near Dark, Elizabeth Holmes
Drift and Pulse, Kathleen Halme
Black Threads, Jeff Friedman
On the Vanishing of Large Creatures, Susan Hutton